To

From

Other books in this series:

HAPPY ANNIVERSARY

To someone special, celebrating your
   LOVELY NEW BABY

To a very special BROTHER

To a very special DAD

To a very special DAUGHTER

To a very special FRIEND

To a very special GRANDMA

To a very special GRANDPA

To a very special GRANDSON

Wishing you HAPPINESS

To my very special HUSBAND

Someone very special...
   TO THE ONE I LOVE

To a very special MOTHER

To a very special SISTER

To a very special SON

To a very special TEACHER

Wishing you happiness
   FOR YOUR WEDDING

To my very special WIFE

Published in 1999 by Helen Exley Giftbooks in Great Britain.
This revised edition published in 2008

12 11 10 9 8 7 6 5 4 3 2 1

ISBN 13: 978-1-84634-267-7

Illustrations and design © Helen Exley 1999, 2008
Important copyright notice: Pam Brown © Helen Exley 1999, 2008
The moral right of the author has been asserted.
A copy of the CIP data is available from the British Library on request.

Acknowledgements: The publishers are grateful for permission to reproduce
copyright material. Whilst every reasonable effort has been made to trace copyright
holders, the publishers would be pleased to hear from any not here acknowledged.
KAHLIL GIBRAN: From The Prophet © 1923 Kahlil Gibran, renewed 1951 by
Administrators C.T.A. of Kahlil Gibran Estate and Mary C. Gibran. ELIZABETH
KUBLER-ROSS: From Soul Gifts in Disguise reprinted in Handbook for the Soul
© 1995 by R. Carson and B. Shield published by Judy Piatkus Ltd. and Little Brown
& Company.
Printed in China.
'TO A VERY SPECIAL'® IS A REGISTERED TRADE MARK OF HELEN EXLEY GIFTBOOKS

Helen Exley Giftbooks, 16 Chalk Hill, Watford, Herts WD19 4BG, UK.
www.helenexleygiftbooks.com

To someone special,
in times of trouble

HOPE AND STRENGTH

EDITED BY HELEN EXLEY
ILLUSTRATED BY JULIETTE CLARKE

I wish that I could ease your pain.
And I hope these words will help
to give you courage and strength
through the difficult times
of your life.

HELEN EXLEY®

Small sadnesses,
great tragedies,
link us all in love

PAM BROWN, b.1928

YOU ARE NOT ALONE

Think of one thing. You are not alone.
A million, million people have known this pain
and found at last a way to new peace.

PAM BROWN, b.1928

Nothing happens to any of us that we are not
formed by nature to bear.

MARCUS AURELIUS (121-180)

The bad news is: ours is an arduous,
long and sometimes tedious journey
through Cesspool Cosmos.
And observe, it is a walk, not a sprint.
The good news is: we are not alone
on this demanding pilgrimage, which means
that some folks we are traveling with make
awfully good models to follow. So, follow them!

CHARLES R. SWINDOLL, FROM "LAUGH AGAIN"

Sorrow is the only one of the lower notes
in the oratorio of our blessedness.

A. J. GORDON

Does the road wind up-hill all the way?
Yes, to the very end.
Will the day's journey take the whole day long?
From morn to night, my friend.

CHRISTINA ROSSETTI (1830-1894)

LESSONS IN LIFE

A person who suffers much, knows much;
every day brings new wisdom.

EWE

Where there is sorrow, where there is pain,
where there is fear,
there loving kindness grows.

PAM BROWN, b.1928

Many of my AIDS patients discovered
that the last year of their lives
was by far their best.
Many have said they wouldn't have traded
the rich quality of that last year of life
for a healthier body.
Sadly, it is only when tragedy strikes
that most of us begin attending
to the deeper aspects of life.

ELIZABETH KÜBLER-ROSS,
FROM "SOUL GIFTS IN DISGUISE"

t is only when we have descended to the depths
of sorrow that we can understand the complexity
of being human,
feel for all other suffering living creatures,
revere courage – and give understanding,
kindness, and companionship to those
who need it.

PAM BROWN, b.1928

A MEDITATION

Deep in the soul, below pain,
below all the distraction of life, is a silence vast
and grand – an infinite ocean of calm,
which nothing can disturb. Nature's own
exceeding peace, which "passes understanding"

C.M.C. QUOTED BY R.M. BUCKE

Do not weep; do not wax indignant.
Understand.

BARUCH SPINOZA

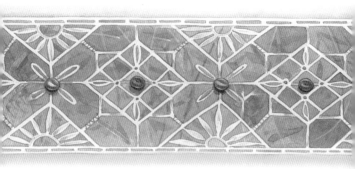

Go with the pain, let it take you...
Open your palms and your body to the pain.
It comes in waves like a tide, and you must be
open as a vessel lying on the beach, letting
it fill you up and then, retreating, leaving
you empty and clear...
With a deep breath –
it has to be as deep as the pain – one reaches
a kind of inner freedom from pain, as though
the pain were not yours but your body's.

ANNE MORROW LINDBERGH (1906-2001)

THE SMALL JOYS

When the world seems huge and dark
and meaningless, focus on little things –
sunlight through leaves, a cat sprawled
across your knees, the taste of an apple,
a dew-bright spider's web.
Time for great wonders later –
now is the time for gentle comforts,
for friendly and familiar things.

PAM BROWN, b.1928

I think these difficult times have helped me to understand better than before how infinitely rich and beautiful life is in every way and that so many things that one goes around worrying about are of no importance whatsoever.

ISAK DINESEN (1885-1962)

Your success and happiness lie in you. External conditions are the accidents of life. The great enduring realities are love and service. Joy is the holy fire that keeps our purpose warm and our intelligence aglow. Resolve to keep happy, and your joy and you shall form an invincible host against difficulty.

HELEN KELLER (1880-1968)

Birds sing after a storm; why shouldn't people feel as free to delight in whatever remains to them?

ROSE KENNEDY

SUFFERING GROWS US

Out of every crisis comes the chance to be
reborn, to reconceive ourselves as
individuals, to choose the kind of change
that will help us to grow and
to fulfil ourselves more completely.

NENA O'NEILL

In the depth of winter, I finally learned
that within me there lay an invincible summer.

ALBERT CAMUS (1913-1960)

THE GREATEST COURAGE

There is the courage that springs from battle fever,

or from a desperate emergency.

And there is a courage that is rooted in

the acceptance of a dreadful circumstance,

and all that it entails –

a courage that brings sanity and cheerfulness

and hope to lives

that could be utterly consumed by sorrow.

This is the courage that endures.

This is the greatest bravery.

PAM BROWN, b.1928

Each handicap is like a hurdle in a steeplechase,

and when you ride up to it,

if you throw your heart over, the horse

will go along, too.

LAWRENCE BIXBY, FROM "COMEBACK FROM
A BRAIN OPERATION"

You have to accept whatever comes
and the only important thing is
that you meet it with courage
and the best that you have to give.

ELEANOR ROOSEVELT (1884-1962)

COURAGE THROUGH THE PAIN

Courage takes many forms.
There is physical courage, there is
moral courage. Then there is a still higher type
of courage – the courage to brave pain,
to live with it, to never let others know of it
and to still find joy in life;
to wake up in the morning
with an enthusiasm for the day ahead.

HOWARD COSELL, FROM "LIKE IT IS"

One of the best safeguards of our hopes
is to be able to mark off the areas
of hopelessness and to acknowledge them,
to face them directly, not with despair
but with the creative intent of keeping
them from polluting
all the areas of possibility.

WILLIAM F. LYNCH

The only courage that matters is the kind
that gets you from one moment to the next.

MIGNON MCLAUGHLIN

You shall be free indeed when your days
are not without a care nor your nights
without a want and a grief.
But rather when these things girdle
your life and yet you rise above them
naked and unbound.

KAHLIL GIBRAN (1883-1931)

IN DEEPEST TROUBLE

If the future seems overwhelming, remember
that it comes one moment at a time.

BETH MENDE CONNY

The best way out is always through.

ROBERT FROST (1874-1963)

The solution is with you. It is as clear and bright
as a flame – but hidden from you by the swirling
dark of misery. Remember all the sweetness
that has been given you – and that still waits
beyond the tumult.

PAM BROWN, b.1928

Even as the stone of the fruit
must break,
that its heart may stand
in the sun, so must
you know pain.

KAHLIL GIBRAN (1883-1931)

It is only when one has been ill and has
recovered that one can properly appreciate
the glory of walking, breathing evenly, sleeping
soundly, seeing clearly, waking to a new day.

PAM BROWN, b.1928

...we may measure our road to wisdom
by the sorrows we have undergone.

BULWER

Once you have been confronted
with a life-and-death situation, trivia
no longer matters. Your perspective grows
and you live at a deeper level.

MARGARETTA "HAPPY" ROCKEFELLER

Out of suffering have emerged the strongest souls,
the most massive characters are seamed with scars....

E.H. CHAPIN

When the worst things happen I will remember
that I can and will handle them. I have
been astounded by the great strength
in myself and in the suffering people
I've known. I see now that there is
unfathomable strength and future joy for me,
whatever awful problems come to me.
And, yes, that the same strength is yours too.

HELEN EXLEY

It will take all your courage to withstand
the onslaught of despair.
But hold to quietness and hope.
ook to the core of your being, the place of peace.

PAM BROWN, b.1928

HOPE

If it were not for hopes, the heart
would break.

THOMAS FULLER (1608-1661),
FROM "DRYAD SONG"

Become a possibilitarian.
No matter how dark things
seem to be or actually are,
raise your sights
and see the possibilities –
always see them, for they're
always there.

NORMAN VINCENT PEALE

Turn your face to the sun
and the shadows
fall behind you.

MAORI PROVERB

It has never been, and never will be easy work!
But the road that is built in hope is more pleasant
to the traveler than the road built in despair, even
though they both lead to the same destination.

MARION ZIMMER BRADLEY

The earth is empty.
The trees, once thick with blossom
stand dead against a bitter sky.
The streams are frozen.
But see – along the branches new buds appear
and greenness pushes through the ground
unnoticed.
Spring may be slow – but will at last return.

PAM BROWN, b.1928

It's better to light a candle than to
curse the darkness.

ELEANOR ROOSEVELT (1884-1962)

A GROWING STRENGTH

Although the world is full of suffering,
it is also full of the overcoming of it.

HELEN KELLER (1880-1968)

To endure is greater than to dare; to tire out
hostile fortune; to be daunted by no difficulty;
to keep heart when all have lost it – who can say
this is not greatness?

WILLIAM MAKEPEACE THACKERAY (1811-1863)

Know how sublime a thing is to suffer
and be strong.

HENRY WADSWORTH LONGFELLOW (1807-1882)

If I were asked to give what I consider the single
most useful bit of advice for all humanity,
it would be this: Expect trouble as an inevitable
part of life, and when it comes, hold your
head high, look it squarely in the eye and say,
'I will be bigger than you. You cannot defeat me."
...Maintaining self-respect in the face of a
devastating experience is of prime importance.

ANN LANDERS

Strengthen me by sympathizing with my strength,
not my weakness.

A. BRONSON ALCOTT

THIS TOO WILL PASS
All shall be well, and all shall be well,
and all manner of things shall be well.

JULIAN OF NORWICH

Weeping may endure for a night,
but the morning brings a shout of joy.

PSALMS 30.5

The shock of failure, of disappointments,
of betrayal, hits like a physical blow.
Breathless and blinded, you lose all contact
with the life you lived till now – the ordinary life
that seemed untouchable.
Hold fast. However impossible it seems that
happiness and certainty will return – they will,
they will. A thousand voices tell you so –
speaking from hard experience.

PAM BROWN, b.1928

"This too will pass..." I was taught these words
by my grandmother as a phrase that is to be used
at all times in your life. When things
are spectacularly dreadful; when things are
absolutely appalling; when everything is superb
and wonderful and marvellous and happy –
say these four words to yourself.
They will give you a sense of perspective....

CLAIRE RAYNER

HAPPINESS WILL ALWAYS BE WITH YOU

The world calls you back to life.

Listen.

The shrill of bird song. The river ice breaking.

Rain after drought. Sunshine after cloud.

PAM BROWN, b.1928

When one door closes another opens.

Expect that new door to reveal even greater

wonders and glories and surprises.

Feel yourself grow with every experience.

EILEEN CADDY

We must live through the dreary winter
if we would value the spring. And the woods
must be cold and silent before the robins sing.
The flowers must be buried in darkness
before they can bud and bloom.
And the sweetest, warmest sunshine comes
after the storm and gloom.

AUTHOR UNKNOWN

The pain passes, but the beauty remains.

PIERRE AUGUSTE RENOIR
(1841-1919),
ON WHY HE STILL PAINTED
DESPITE PAINFUL ARTHRITIS

Walk on a rainbow trail;
walk on a trail of song,
and all about you will be beauty.
There is a way out of every dark mist,
over a rainbow trail.

NAVAJO SONG